Two on a Bridge

A Guidebook Using Ancient Insight to Unleash the Healing Powers that Surround Us

by
Linda L. Stampoulos

CCB Publishing
British Columbia, Canada

Two on a Bridge: A Guidebook Using Ancient Insight to Unleash the Healing Powers that Surround Us

Copyright ©2011 by Linda L. Stampoulos
ISBN-13 978-1-926918-64-8
First Edition

Library and Archives Canada Cataloguing in Publication
Stampoulos, Linda L., 1946-
Two on a bridge : a guidebook using ancient insight to unleash the healing powers that surround us / written by Linda L. Stampoulos.
ISBN 978-1-926918-63-1 (bound).--ISBN 978-1-926918-64-8 (pbk.)
Also available in electronic format.
1. Self-actualization (Psychology). 2. Spiritual life. I. Title.
BF637.S4S71 2011   158.1   C2011-904195-2

For all general information regarding other books, visit pompanobooks.com

Original cover art design by Jinger Heaston: www.jingraphix.org

Extreme care has been taken to ensure that all information presented in this book is accurate and up to date at the time of publishing. Neither the author nor the publisher can be held responsible for any errors or omissions. Additionally, neither is any liability assumed for damages resulting from the use of the information contained herein.

All rights reserved. No part of this publication may be reproduced, stored in a retrieval system or transmitted in any form or by any means, electronic, mechanical, photocopying, recording or otherwise without the express written permission of the publisher. Printed in the United States of America and the United Kingdom.

Publisher: CCB Publishing
             British Columbia, Canada
             www.ccbpublishing.com

Dedication

*"Every one of us has to face that day,
do you cross the bridge or fade away?"**

This book is dedicated to everyone who struggles with life's challenges and is not afraid to reach out to the hidden powers that are waiting to help them on their journey across the bridge.

* "The Bridge" lyrics by Elton John and Bernie Taupin.
<u>The Captain and The Kid</u>, Mercury Records, 2006.

Other Books by Linda L. Stampoulos

Visiting the Grand Canyon, Views of Early Tourism

The Redemption of Black Elk

Black Elks Vermachtnis

Two on a Bridge
(Guidebook & Workbook)

Contents

Welcome to the Bridge vi

Part I: Getting Started 1

The Invitation 4
Session 1: The Power of the Place 5
Session 2: The Powers of the Vision Hoop 7
Session 3: The Vision Hoop: The Power Over Demons 10
Session 4: The Vision Hoop: The Power From
    Your Center 13
Session 5: The Ghost Dance: The Power to
    Strengthen Belief 16
Session 6: The Ghost Dance: Power to Survive 19
Session 7: Stepping off the Bridge 22

Part II: Readings for Discussion 24

The Vision Hoop: The Circle of Winters 25
The Thunder-Beings Speak 27
The People on the Bus 29
The Tiospaye at the Little Bighorn 31
Demon or Dragon? 35
But the Tigers Come at Night 37
The Ghost Dance 39
The Bloody Snow 42
Excerpt from: *The Lost Journal of Tatanka Chante* 46
Behold the Earth, For across it are Two Roads 50
Two on a Bridge: The Guideposts 53

Welcome to the Bridge

The bridge has always been a powerful metaphor representing a path connecting one place to another. Throughout our lives we make numerous "crossings" some easier than others. Too often the journey becomes burdened by everyday problems that depress us, drag us down, and require tremendous amounts of energy. We prefer they would just go away but any rational person knows they won't. Like some itch you can't quite scratch, they constantly keep demanding our attention. Often the mire and the muck we find ourselves in require more energy to cope than we alone can give.

We can, however, obtain some measure of relief. The burden of life's problems doesn't have to be as debilitating as it perhaps seems to be right now. Volumes have been written to address personal problems and dedicate themselves to the theme of "self help." This guidebook can be another approach to healing. It picks up where "self help" leaves off. Through guided discussion, you and someone you choose will meet and explore the problematic issues in your lives and at the same time, learn about the ancient powers and energy sources that surround us today.

The basic concept is quite simple:

Strength and healing can be enhanced when two join together, share a short journey, and discover the healing energy that can come from the power of two.

To help you, there are Guideposts along the way that present the principles you will need to follow to successfully navigate the bridge. You will also benefit from the insight of Joseph Campbell, one of the world's foremost authorities on ancient cultures, as well as the work of the psychologist, Carl Jung whose research examined the source of such ancient power, but until now, left its application to our everyday lives hidden in deep narrative.

You will also be guided by the message and legacy of Black Elk, whose own life was truly a journey. He lived some one hundred and thirty-five years ago, and as a young child of the Oglala Lakota Sioux, Black Elk had been given a vision; a mighty vision which would lead him on a personal journey intended to result in the peace and flourishing of his people. With the help of his vision, Black Elk was able to unfold symbols and metaphors in very unique ways so that the lessons learned built on one another and, in the end, laid out before us an ancient path toward inner strength and a balanced life.

Perhaps the most powerful symbol associated with Black Elk is his vision hoop, pictured on the cover of this guidebook. In the pages that follow you will become more familiar with the vision hoop, and come to see it as a source of energy and power. As you travel across the bridge and follow the guideposts, the ancient sources of power will begin to become clearer and more applicable to your life. Keep in mind, the origins of this power remains a great mystery.

There is nothing new here; basic truths that exist throughout time. The challenge is to lift those meanings from one generation into another so that in re-examining them we too may have the direction, a way for us to go. But as with most elements of our lives, the destination is secondary. It is the journey that involves us most. How we travel through our days, as well as the direction we choose to take are really most important.

Guidepost
One principle is certain, if you step on to the bridge and follow its guideposts, you will not be the same person who steps off at the end.

PART I
Getting Started

Part I of this Guidebook presents the steps you and your partner will take to achieve your goals. It is divided into seven sessions. Each will review a source of power and offer a list of suggested readings for you to prepare for the next session with your partner.

Part II is a collection of Readings for Discussion that offer greater insight and real life application of the many powers available to us. In addition to this guidebook you will benefit from having the companion workbook. The workbook suggests activities you and your partner will complete during your time together. These activities are designed to help you access the different energy sources and hopefully make them a part of your life.

The process is quite simple. It involves a series of meetings accompanied by time each will spend alone for reflection. There is work to do together and also work you will do alone.

Guidepost

Maintain your own special place, a base location just for you alone. Your meditation here will begin with a certain state of mind, a level of awareness which will eventually lead itself to its own energy source.

The first step on your journey is to provide yourself with a base, your own personal setting, an actual location from which you can begin. This place is just for you alone, without your partner. If your life is like most, your day begins at the sound of your alarm, you get ready for work, do the shopping, balance the check book; as the demands of our lives go on and on. There is ALWAYS something required of us to do. More often we get so involved in our everyday activities that we hardly know where we are. The claims of the environment can be so great, most of our actions are economically or socially determined and so very demanding. These things do not come out of our life, they penetrate into it.

Selection of your special place varies from person to person. In general it's best if it is outdoors, close to a natural setting. Nature provides subliminal triggers, ancient triggers, firing energy into memory cells gone dormant. These "sparks" will ignite a nostalgic mood, familiar yet unfamiliar, imprinted wiring that will lend itself to deeper thought or insight.

You will begin your meditation with a certain state of mind, a level of awareness which will eventually lead itself to its own energy source. Joseph Campbell referred to this as a level of consciousness, something beyond awareness. It is a connection to a greater consciousness beyond that of one's own and shared by all. It will be as strong and as deep as you allow yourself to move into it. Everyone has the capacity to move from their everyday happenings into this other place, a place where your mind and body want to go. No one can tell you where your serenity is, everyone must learn to recognize it on their own. But when you even have a small recognition of where it lies, "grab it" says Campbell, and you will put yourself on a track that has been there waiting for you all the time.

Meditation places individual awareness on a higher

platform allowing one to "listen to the body's own spirituality and heart life." This life song is inside each of us. "The world is full of people," Campbell goes on, "who have stopped listening to themselves." They go with society's demands and live a life that their inner voice is not interested in at all. To live a full life one must appreciate the mysterious forces that not only surround us but run through us. Call it what you will: spirit, energy, power, consciousness, Chi, the idea is the same: this "life force" is in every living thing, animal and plant. One key to a full and balanced life is understanding how to recognize and manage this power. A person need not realize the FULL nature of such a life source, indeed many people live their entire lives on a "hit and miss" approach, not really knowing or grasping its full potential.

To somehow connect to such a power is a primary goal. It begins when a person consciously puts himself in a setting conducive to apprehending the experience. Remember, the energy is there, one just needs to be able to connect with it. Joseph Campbell felt it was absolutely necessary that a person make time and take time to be completely alone, separated from the daily grind of endless demands, and enter a special place. This special place according to Joseph Campbell, is an absolute necessity for anybody today. It can be a certain time of day when you can visit to remove yourself from the world around you. When you are there, you don't know what's in the newspapers, you don't concern yourself with your finances or the other thoughts that can invade your peacefulness. This is a place of creative incubation, he states, a place where you can experience and bring forth what you are or what you might be.

It can be as simple as listening to your favorite music, reading the book you've always wanted, or even closing your eyes and shutting out the noise of the world. At first nothing happens, but he assures us, if you have a special place and learn to use it, something will happen. You will begin to get the "thou" feeling of life.

The Indians of the Plains lived in a world of nature and experienced its tremendous power all the time. Campbell notes, "Just being there, you feel the wonder and you become aware of something larger than the human personification of the energies that exist."

The security of a special place can be comforting. It serves as a warm retreat from the often harsh realities of our world. It is important to remember, though, that one MUST venture out into the world again to meet today's challenges. One could think of it as temporary oasis, giving us the opportunity for reflection and renewal as we make our life journey.

The Invitation

To begin, you need to select a partner, someone who will accompany you on your journey across the bridge. The individual you select is entirely your choice. It should be someone you feel comfortable with, someone you trust, and especially someone who is a good listener. Invite them to share some time, usually one meeting a week for about seven weeks. During this period, you both will explore the activities, the suggested readings, and become familiar with the powers that surround us. The bridge becomes a platform for discussion as you make your way across.

And so your journey across the bridge begins.

Session One
The Power of the Place

<u>Guidepost</u>
Maintain a consistent place to meet with your partner. As this place becomes more familiar, it will eventually produce a power source of its own.

The next step is for you and your partner to select a place to meet. Selecting a place to meet may appear a casual request, but it is really very important. This place will eventually produce a power source of its own. It will supply the spark to ignite the beacons of your thoughts and the energy to sustain and enrich them. Decide on this together. Pick a place that will always be available and has privacy. Depending on both your situations, it should as convenient a location as possible. The design is to meet once a week for a number of weeks, both of you can decide on a schedule that fits into your life.

<u>Guidepost</u>
After each meeting with your partner, return to your own special place for reflection.

Keep in mind, to get the most out of your journey together, you must use the time in between meetings to reflect on your last session together. Use the Workbook to jot your thoughts while still fresh in your mind. As someone once wrote, "The time we spend together is worth the time alone."

As mentioned, Part II of this Guidebook is a collection of Suggested Readings for Discussion. At the end of each session, is a list of these to read in preparation for your next session.

Suggested Readings for Session Two
    The Vision Hoop: The Circle of Winters
    Thunder-Beings Speak

Session Two
The Powers of the Vision Hoop

After you have selected your special place and become familiar with the peaceful reflection and solitude it affords, you are ready to explore the next source of power. It involves the image of a circle, or vision hoop. The term comes from a vision given to a young Oglala Lakota Sioux named Black Elk. His vision revealed powers that surround us, even today. There are many powers involving the use of the vision hoop and the image of the circle.

Joseph Campbell often referred to the power symbolized by the circle. It represents a totality, he explained, a unit with no beginning and no end. It is an ever-present thing, the center from which you have come and back to where you go. For your personal journey, the concept of the circle is one in which you will learn the powers available to you, and how to use them.

Guidepost
Think of your life as a circle containing all the elements of your world both positive and negative.

Joseph Campbell tells us, the circle can be thought of as the psychological expression of the totality of one's self. Simply stated, circles shut out the outside and hold in the inside.

Two on a Bridge

When you are in your special place, you are asked to think of your immediate concerns, both positive and negative. These are concerns that immediately affect your life, whether or not you have control over them. The Workbook will ask you to list the elements of your life that are of most concern to you and which are at least to some degree, under your control. This exercise accomplishes two things: first it delimits the issues you need to address and are most on your mind (containment); and second, it blocks out those more distant issues that are beyond your control (protection).

Your circle, or vision hoop then, is in effect you. It gives you a oneness, a whole being. The focus now becomes inward. The hoop's containment gives you a feeling of control. By definition you are now able to see exactly what you must face. The issues shrink to fit inside and become more manageable and less overwhelming. It is through these concepts of "shrinkage" and "containment" that the elements of your life are reduced to their proper proportions.

This is no easy task. In the beginning your hoop will contain many issues beyond your control. Throughout the day we face issues ranging from our local arena to world events well beyond our locus of control. It is our nature to take on the problems of the world in an effort to do good. Drawing the hoop of containment does not mean that broader issues will be ignored. On the contrary, the exercise is meant to build a good base where one can construct inner strength and have a solid place to move out into the world again.

To quote Carl Jung's description, "the circle is the most powerful religious symbol, it is one of the great primeval images of mankind; in considering the circle, you are analyzing yourself."

Guidepost
Throughout your day your must constantly decide whether or not an issue is a positive or negative force. If it is positive keep it close to you and nourish it. If it is negative, try not to concentrate on it, this gives it energy and strength.

    Jung believed that the totality or the content of your circle comprises all the issues you are aware of (consciousness), and a personal unconsciousness which he defines as chiefly those issues which at one time have been conscious but which have disappeared from consciousness through having been forgotten or repressed. It is the combination of the conscious and the personal unconscious that Jung refers to as "the self" and claims both exist within the circle you have drawn.

    We continue our journey of exploration by looking inward, secure in the knowledge that we have the peace and protection of our vision hoop.

Suggested Readings for Session Three
    The People on the Bus
    The Tiospaye at the Little Bighorn

Session Three
The Vision Hoop:
The Power Over Demons

<u>Guidepost</u>
You will never be totally free from negative forces. There will always be demons invading your circle. Do our best to recognize them for what they represent, and keep them as far from your center as possible.

    Knowing we are not alone is a source of comfort as we continue to go through life. Our journey is made much easier knowing that someone else is there, sharing our joys and our sorrows. Sometimes it helps to think of those gone before, who traveled our same path and serve as models for our life.
    Joseph Campbell often referred to the hero and the hero path. "A hero," he tells us, "is someone who has found something or done something beyond the normal range of achievement and experience. He has given his life to something bigger than himself." This, he explains, could be in terms of a physical deed, such as the brave acts of Crazy Horse; or, a spiritual deed, such as Black Elk's devotion to the fulfillment of his vision. But there is always a price to pay; the hero has sacrificed himself for the betterment of others.
    Our next step on our journey across the bridge involves

examination of the contents of your vision hoop. While in your place of solitude and peace, you were asked to draw a circle containing your immediate concerns. Now you are to examine these concerns and determine whether they add to your life or take away from it. Keep in mind, your hoop contains both positive and negative elements: heroes and demons. This process of arranging the forces inside you compares to Jung's use of the *mandala*, the Sanskrit word meaning circle. He often would have his clients draw their mandala, and use it as an instrument of contemplation. Campbell tells us that the organizing of feelings and issues within the mandala is an instinctive expression of human desire to create organization from chaos and to address the confusing flux of inner and outer life.

Guidepost
You must learn to manage your demons, because some of them will always exist. But you must slay your dragons because you are the one who created them.

You begin by placing your issues in some kind of order, always keeping the positive ones close and the negative ones toward the rim, away from the center. You are also asked to name them. Are they your heroes or your demons? "Naming" has a control power in itself. When casting out a demon, Jesus called it by name (Mark, Chapter 5). Identification reduces the perceived strength of the negative force and gives you more control over its power. It no longer can feed on your fear. In the same way, those positive forces become more prominent, giving you a strength you never realized you had. No one will ever be totally free from negative forces. There will always be demons invading your circle. We must do our best to recognize them for what they represent, and keep them as far from our center as possible.

By repeating this exercise you will begin to become more and more aware of an unconsciousness that lies deep within. Visiting the quietness of your special place, drawing your hoop of containment limiting your concerns, the identification of your heroes and demons, are early steps toward self discovery. Each experience will bring increased inner strength because you are in control of the conflicting forces within each of us. Slowly the forces locked inside will emerge and you will position them within your sacred hoop. You are becoming coordinated with the greater consciousness of the universe. As Campbell says, "All that is unconscious is dangerous and powerful and must be controlled by consciousness. The hero transcends his humanity and associates himself with the powers of nature which are the true powers of our life and from which our mind removes us." Only through self discovery and meditation do we leave the distractions and worldly demands, and turn our sights inward, unlocking who we really are and what we really can become.

Guidepost
When you are not in your special place, remember the positive thoughts and call on them when you need a burst of energy and joy.

Suggested Reading for Session Four
    Demon or Dragon?

Session Four
The Vision Hoop: The Power From Your Center

The first sections of this book encourage you to coordinate and order the forces that affect you everyday. It was recommended that you place the negative forces as far away as possible, close to the rim of your hoop. This process prevents them from gaining access to the energy of the center, the source of psychic power. Prior to the positioning the issues within your hoop you had to determine if they were positive or negative. The more positive the force, the closer it was placed to your center.

But this is where the thought process and the mind's influence end. Campbell reminds us that the brain is a secondary organ and must not put itself in control. It must submit to serve the humanity of the body. As one reaches his true center, the mind's involvement in assigning a value to the issue is no longer at work, neither positive nor negative forces prevail. Arrival at the true center establishes a psychic connection to something greater than one's self. A stream of energy runs through the center, axis mundi, from bottom to top. The whirlpool of positive and negative forces continue to spin around inside the hoop, but the individual who has found his center leaves his thought process behind and begins to feel what Campbell calls the "thou" feeling of life.

The discovery of your center will happen when you are in your special place. Once you find your center, it becomes a source of psychic energy, you become one in accord with the inevitability of your life. You begin to live with a knowledge of life's mystery, giving you a zest and a new balance. As your anxieties begin to ease, you will see the positive values becoming clearer. Unless your center is found, you are torn apart. You listen closer to the system that dominates you than to yourself.

We are so accustomed to living within the rules of a system. The demands of which, Campbell tells us, can eat you up and cause you to lose your humanity. Although we can't always change the system, he advises us to find a way to live within the system as a human being. We do this, he says, by resisting the system's impersonal claims. If a person doesn't listen to the needs of his own spiritual and heart life and insist on a certain program, the person has aligned himself with a programmatic life, one that his body is not interested in at all.

Guidepost

When you are alone, concentrate on your feelings, develop an inner focus that reveals a central point inside of you. This energy source is found by your heart, not your head.

Jung tells us that in the center of the circle there is a conscious self-awareness and balance. He says that every person has an innate tendency to pursue this inner harmony which aligns the conscious with the personal unconscious in a psychic connection.

Have you ever experienced a psychic connection? It is a

connection to something bigger than yourself. You may have experienced it and never realized what it was. Often this connection or communication comes through the senses. It could be the feeling that comes when you are walking on a beach, feeling the power of the wind, or experiencing the smell of something that triggers a lost memory. It leaves you with a feeling of a connection, a yielding acknowledgment of something that has gone before and yet continues to present itself as a dominant force. This joins you with the collective power of those who have gone before and those not yet born.

<u>Suggested Readings for Session Five</u>
    But the Tigers Come at Night
    The Ghost Dance

Session Five
The Ghost Dance: The Power to Strengthen Belief

Another source of power that has its origin in ancient cultures is the personal strength and energy that comes with a connection to those who have passed away. It is something everyone has in common, and unless you really think about it, it doesn't always present itself as something real, not to mention powerful. We often gain strength from remembering our loved ones who are no longer with us. Their memory can bring a smile and when needed, a source strength. We know it really isn't them giving us the energy, it is our memory of them when they were here. We can even remember the sound of their voice and what they would say and do in different situations. It can be very comforting and very powerful.

To understand the next power source you will need to step back in time, about 125 years, and relive the experience of the Sioux Indians following their victory at the Battle of the Little Bighorn. For many of the western Indian tribes, the Ghost Dance proved to be a powerful connection to the dead. For the Sioux Indians the Ghost Dance promised that they would again rise to power and with the help of the dead, they would reclaim the land; the buffalo would return, and they would be free. It promised all these things would come to pass in a short time.

Within ten years after their victory at the Little Bighorn,

the U.S. Calvary hunted the Indians and made them relocate onto reservation land. Those who resisted scattered and hid. Reservation life was forced upon them and the Indians, who for their entire lives hunted and followed the buffalo, were now struggling to reconcile themselves to the ways of a new civilization. Hungry, desperate and depressed, the people searched in vain for a center, a focus for their lives. They began to follow the teachings of a messiah, a Paiute named Wovoka who spread the Ghost Dance movement. One might say that the Ghost Dance became everyone's last chance at returning hope in these desperate times. By connecting to those "ghosts" or that spirit army who had gone before, they would have them return to join the effort, to recapture dreams, and to bring back their old way of life.

Guidepost
The power doesn't necessarily come from those who have died, rather it comes from the belief in the power of the connection.

For the Indian people, the Ghost Dance movement was a promise, one that would return the old ways, the spirits of the dead, and the buffalo. For some it became their belief system. In ten short years everything they cherished had been taken away. Their children were sent to boarding schools in the East, their food was rationed and they had to wait in line for supplies. Treaties with the government were broken, and most important, the buffalo had all but disappeared.

Then, by some miracle, a messiah came and promised them a power, an energy and strength that made them invincible. The power was coming from their belief in the connection to those gone before. They had faith in that connection, and they danced and sang songs of power and resurrection. Isn't that the power of belief? Isn't that what faith can do?

Guidepost
Belief helps us to understand that there is an invisible plain behind the visible one, supporting us with energy. Faith is designed to put our mind in accord with our body and our way of life in accord with the way nature designs.

Suggested Readings for Session Six
    The Bloody Snow
    The Lost Journal of Tatanka Chante

Session Six
The Ghost Dance: Power to Survive

This new Ghost Dance movement threatened the army who controlled the Reservations, and subsequently order came for the Indians to stop the Dance. Despite the orders, the Indians continued the movement. For Black Elk's people, the Ghost Dance movement promised a return to the old ways; an opportunity for the individual to return to a place of pride, a place where they could feel good about themselves. Yet it was more than that, it was the courage to face unimaginable odds and still survive. As Mooney described when he told about the babies living through the harsh weather after Wounded Knee, "The tenacity of life so characteristic of indigenous people was strikingly illustrated in the case of these wounded and helpless women and children who thus lived three days through a Dakota blizzard, without food, shelter, or attention to their wounds."

A baby survived four days alone in a blizzard! Nothing we ever face will compare to what the Sioux Indians experienced during their last years of freedom. What power sustained them during the massacre? How were they able to survive a blizzard? Many say this is all part of the Great Mystery, the unknown power that surrounds us. Our quest then is to acknowledge this mystery and seek to discover its power: that burning point, that becoming point when you are fearless and desireless, not driven by need or want, but by the energy that comes from within.

Another universal message of power and courage comes from the Ghost Dance. A cottonwood tree was in the center of the dance, and was nourished by the energy of their center. Its direction of strength ran from bottom to top connecting with the forces and energy of the center. It was *waken*, sacred, and it held a place of high honor. Black Elk continually referenced the Sacred Tree of his vision, and emphasized its need to be nourished. He knew it represented his people's connection with their inner self and they must learn of its dimension. The true person waiting to be discovered, had to be found. What's more, it had to be encouraged to grow and blossom. This is not an easy task. It takes a courage of conviction, one easily forfeited to the demands of this world. The metaphor of the "tree" epitomized the renaissance that was about to begin. Everyone felt it; everyone believed it.

The custom of a circle dance centering around a tree is common to other cultures. In parts of Germany, May 1st is an especially important day. In German villages, it has been the custom for centuries to cut a tall and straight tree, the Maibaum (May Tree), a day or two before May 1 and place it in the middle of the village. It was decorated with a wreath of Spring flowers and colorful ribbons. The traditional Maypole dance has an even number of dancers facing alternatively clockwise and counterclockwise. They move in a circle in the direction they are facing raising and passing the ribbons they hold. The elements are always the same across cultures, a celebration, a dance in a circle, and a tree in the center.

Joseph Campbell tells us that the symbol of the tree is present in many religions. Christ died on the tree of the cross and was born to the spirit; and the Buddha sits under the tree of knowledge and immortal life. The imagery gives one the realization that there is a higher plain and the body is a vehicle. It is clear to Campbell that Black Elk's vision was part of a "shamanic experience." For the shaman, all that exists in the revealed world has a living force within it. This life energy force is conceived as a divine force which permeates all. The knowledge that life is power is the realization of the shaman.

Another interpretation of the imagery of the tree and the mystery of the shaman is presented by Joan Halifax. From their visions and dreams, shamans describe a "cosmic tree" which is a symbol of perpetual regeneration. It is this tree with its life-giving waters that binds all realms together, the roots of the tree penetrate the depths of the Underworld. The body of the tree transects the Middle World, and the crown embraces the heavens. This great tree stands at the very center of the universe directing the vision of a culture skyward towards the eternally sacred.

On an individual level, the tree represents a person's potential, coming from the center, it is the true core of their life's purpose. Nourishing it and helping it "bloom" becomes a process of self-realization, coming in touch with the real meaning and intent of one's life. For Black Elk's people, the Ghost Dance Religion promised a return to the old ways; an opportunity for the individual to return to a place of pride, a place where they could again feel good about themselves.

Suggested Reading for Session Seven
Behold the Earth, for across it are Two Roads

Session Seven
Stepping off the Bridge

Congratulations!

You have completed your journey and are about to step off the bridge. Hopefully you have a better understanding of the ancient powers that surround us. Through guided discussion you and your partner explored some of the problematic issues in your lives and with the help of the activities in the Workbook, you both are now able to take advantage of the "hidden hands" that are here to help you. By spending time in your special place, you will continue to recognize your own depths and gain that deep sense of inner peace and understanding.

Concentration on your inner self will point the way to who you are and the potential of what you really can become. The final steps of your journey across the bridge leads you to the most critical step, one that involves the highest level of fulfillment: self-actualization. Self-actualizing persons repeatedly experience awe, pleasure, and wonder in their everyday world. In varying degrees, they have feelings of wonder with limitless horizons opening up, followed by a conviction that the experience was important and must carryover into everyday life. They have a deep feeling of empathy, sympathy, and compassion for human beings in general. Most important, this feeling is unconditional. And finally, the self-actualizing person is highly ethical and willing to learn from anyone.

One might say that the Red Road is actually the road to

self-actualization. In terms of your personal journey, the Red Road represents a choice or direction for you to go.

You have the guideposts. You have the promise of the vision hoop. And, for a time, you had the comfort that comes from sharing time with a friend. Above all, you have the advantage of knowing the ancient energies that surround us, and most important, you have the nourishment that comes from the power of two.

Part II
Readings for Discussion

This section of the Guidebook offers a collection of readings meant to highlight the guideposts and principles of Part I. They are meant to prepare you and your partner for the coming session, beginning with session two. The workbook can be used to enhance the readings with questions to guide your discussion.

Suggested Readings for Session Two
    The Vision Hoop: The Circle of Winters
    The Thunder-Beings Speak

Suggested Readings for Session Three
    The People on the Bus
    The Tiospaye at the Little Bighorn

Suggested Reading for Session Four
    Demon or Dragon?

Suggested Readings for Session Five
    But the Tigers Come at Night
    The Ghost Dance

Suggested Readings for Session Six
    The Bloody Snow
    The Lost Journal of Tatanka Chante

Suggested Reading for Session Seven
    Behold the Earth, for across it are Two Roads

The Vision Hoop: The Circle of Winters

Another source of power involves the image of a circle, often referred to as the vision hoop, pictured on the cover of this Guidebook. The term comes from a vision given to a young Oglala Lakota Sioux named Black Elk. His vision revealed powers that surround us, even today. There are many powers involving the use of the vision hoop and the image of the circle.

The colors making up the outside circle of the hoop explain our life journey, it is our circle of winters. Tracing the colors in a clockwise direction describes the stages we pass through as we grow old. The sun rises in the East (yellow) and here we begin our journey. Black Elk tells us, the South (red) is the source of life for the sun lives there. A man advances from there toward the setting sun of his life. As men and things grow older, they move toward the setting sun where all things pass. The West (black) is the greatest source of power, probably because as men get older they get wisdom. As they get older they approach the colder North (white) where the grey hairs are. And does he not then arrive, if he lives, at the source of light and understanding which is the East (yellow), and completing the circle with the sun does he not return to where he began, to give back his life to all life, and his flesh to the earth whence it came.

When discussing the features of the circle Joseph Campbell points out that its own geometry indicates a journey. The line travels around going out and down and around back to where you started. It represents a total journey but on inspection has no beginning and no end.

The Thunder-Beings Speak

Imagine a hot, clear summer day on the Great Plains. Without warning, the sky suddenly darkens, flashes of light strike the tops of the cottonwood trees, setting them ablaze. At the same time sheets of hail, the size of golf balls batter the ground. Fire and ice from the same angry storm. To the Sioux Indians these were Spirit forms, hard to understand yet very powerful. They were *wakan*. These Thunder-beings who controlled the fire and the ice had both the power to kill and the power to heal. According to Black Elk, from this water all healing herbs grow.

When people of the twenty-first century experience violent storms, one of their first concerns is the interruption of power and the many inconveniences of having to do without electricity for a time. The wonder and magnificence of nature is often lost to the complaint of a "missed" television program or a scramble for candles so often misplaced after the last storm. Powerful thunderstorms cannot be ignored no matter when or where you live. They can make you stop whatever you are doing, even for a minute, and recognize a power that exists, one that is beyond our control.

The Indians of the Plains, however, lived in a world of nature and experienced its tremendous power all the time. Campbell notes, "just being there, you feel the wonder and you become aware of something larger than the human personification of the energies that exist."

He goes on to say that we all have basic needs and that the realization of these needs guides us inward to our "bliss station," a place of peace and self-realization. This is a place where we can develop a discipline for pulling all those scattered aspects of ourselves and putting an order to them. Upon continually returning to our special place we eventually rise up to a higher platform, a higher spiritual plain. The forces of society may try to lower our sights, but once there is a realization of who we are in this place, there is an explosion of self-worth and higher consciousness. We begin to live in terms of who we believe we are, not who or what society tells us we should be.

The security of a special place can be comforting. It serves as a warm retreat from the often harsh realities of our world. It is important to remember, though, that one MUST venture out into the world again to meet today's challenges. One could think of it as temporary oasis, giving us the opportunity for reflection and renewal as we make our life journey.

The People on the Bus

For a moment, let's consider you are a bus driver. You have many people on your bus and you can keep your eye on them in your rearview mirror. Now let's suppose that each person on the bus represents either a positive or a negative force in your life. The positive individuals you'll tend to keep toward the front of the bus, close to you. The negative ones you'll push toward the back of the bus away from you. These shadow figures will exist in the back of the bus, the region Jung refers to as the unconscious.

This arrangement may seem like a solution at first, but then you realize that the shadows in the back keep moving closer to the front demanding your attention. You watch them in your mirror and often you become distracted. As they move closer, they confront a personal consciousness, you the driver. The shadows can be so disturbing that they more often get repressed into the unconscious. You also come to realize that keeping these shadows in the back requires a great deal of energy, constant energy, because the minute you let down your guard, they begin to creep up again. Pushing the shadows to the back, repressing them, represents a vanishing level of consciousness, it weakens them and they increasingly lack the power to express and assert themselves. However, there is a price to pay. As Jung continues, repression would protect the shadows from vanishing, because repressed feelings have the very best chance of survival, as we know from experience that nothing is corrected in the unconscious. The shadows just remain dormant until your energy level is exhausted and they find their way back into your thoughts.

As your day goes on, you find you are becoming more and

more tired and you no longer have the energy to push them to the back of the bus. At some point you will need to make a decision: do you want to go on the way you are, repressing the negative forces, the shadows in your life, or do you want to slowly bring them forward, face them and eventually get them off the bus.

The Tiospaye at the Little Bighorn

In June of 1876, a few days before America would mark its Centennial Celebration, a gathering of Indian people made history in a rich valley on the Little Bighorn River. Their legacy consists not of a victory in battle, but in the events that happened in the weeks prior to the arrival of Custer and his troops.

It was Spring, in the Moon When the Ponies Shed, a time to celebrate new life and freedom, to follow the buffalo and other game. Men, women and children came to thank the Creator, *Wakan Tanka*, for safely bringing them through the harsh winter. They camped in the place where from ages past, they called the "Greasy Grass," a place of solitude and worship. There were a few lodges at first, but over a period of weeks, the gathering, often referred to as *Tiospaye*, or the Golden Encampment, would grow to become the largest in recorded American history. Eyewitnesses reported there being over 1,000 lodges, each leader with his own camp circle, with up to 7,000 people, almost 1,500 of them warriors. Among the many tribes represented, were the Yanktonais, Cheyenne, Arapaho and of the Lakota Sioux: the Oglala, Hunkpapa, Sicangu, Miniconjou, Itazipco, Siha Sapa, and Oohenumpa. It is said that their tipi circles went from south to north.

There was a powerful majesty surrounding the people in attendance, strong leaders who protected the tribes: Crazy Horse, Gall, American Horse, He Dog and their camp circles were joined as one statement of freedom. Black Elk was 13 years old at that time. It was four years earlier that, by a strange coincidence, his family was camped at this very site and he received his great vision and the message of the vision hoop.

During the day Black Elk recounts, the elders would sit in Counsel, women would dig turnips and prepare meals, the children swam in the river and rode their ponies. After dark, the drums would echo the heartbeat of the dancers and tales would be told victories and of the old ways. As Black Elk explained to Joseph Epes Brown,

> I should tell you why the drum is important to us. It is because the round form of the drum represents the whole universe, and its steady strong beat is the pulse, the heart, throbbing at the center of the universe. It is the voice of *Wakan Tanka*, and this sound stirs us and helps us to understand the mystery and the power of all things.

"The round form of the drum representing the universe," another example of the importance of the symbol of a circle. Not only was there a totality represented, but a source of power coming in the form of a drum beat.

The evening fires of Tiospaye would burn late into the night. The full moon made it seem like daylight and the dancing could go on forever. Never before was there such a feeling of confidence and freedom. From Sitting Bull's vision, they knew they were invincible. The following describes, June 25, 1876, the morning of the Custer battle as the tribes were experiencing the restful slumber, sleeping in circles of harmony and peace:

> The golden sun of a new day slowly pushes its brilliance into a waiting June morning. Mists of a cool

night now meeting the warmth of dawn hang as if artistically draped by the Creator between the spirit world and mother earth. Flickering eerily across the landscape are the dying embers of the campfires of *Tiospaye*. It is quiet. It is peaceful. It is deceiving.

Majestic, regal, strong and stoic Sitting Bull stares ominously across the horizon on which land his people still peacefully and rhythmically slumber. One can only imagine the pain and grief and suffering within the holy man's heart as deep within he knows what others know not: it is the night not the dawn which lies ahead. It is the end not the beginning which the rising sun symbolizes on this June morning.

Off in the distance is the silent sound of thunder; not of the heavens but of earth; not of nature but of man. He hears not through his ears but through his spirit. Never again will his people gather and celebrate as they have just done. Never again will the freedom fires of Tiospaye burn so brightly among so many. It is dawn, but the time grows short. It is the day, but the night draws near. They will be victorious in the battle against Custer, but with that victory would come the last days of the vision hoop.

The tribe's sacred hoop was usually entrusted to the medicine man. Coming from a long line of these healers, Black Elk was very familiar with its power and meaning. In his 1896 report for the Smithsonian Institutes' Bureau of Ethnology entitled "The Ghost Dance Religion and the Sioux Outbreak of 1890" James Mooney stated that the medicine man of Big Foot's band carried such a hoop with him in their flight from the north, and displayed it at every dance held by the band until the fatal day of Wounded Knee.

Black Elk saw that outside elements were responsible for the breaking of the oneness and wholeness his people enjoyed. Large scale disruption began after the Indian victory at the Little Bighorn. However, Black Elk continued to believe the positive message of his vision. That there is not one hoop, but many hoops representing many nations and people of all colors. There is a promise of salvation for all people within the harmony of the sacred hoop. The challenge is to find a way to nourish the spiritual needs of a people while they search after their own uniqueness, their own identity in the modern world.

To continue our journey then, we must keep to Black Elk's message, concentrate on our own oneness, our own hoop.

Demon or Dragon?

Carl Jung tells of a young woman who came to see him for psychiatric help. She said she felt alone in the world and at times very afraid. He asked her to draw a picture of her feelings, and when she would return for her next visit, she could explain her drawing.

Upon her return the woman showed her picture. She painted herself as a figure stuck in the rocks with waves cracking down on her. Among the rocks were boulders that looked like "hard-boiled eggs cut in two with a golden yolk in the middle." He asked her to try again and she did. This time there were bolts of lightning hitting the rocks and breaking open these golden globes.

After several counseling sessions he explained to her that the boulders were her dragons, formed by her own mind. The liberating flash of lightning that broke open the boulders was a symbol of a realization that came from their discussions that showed she wasn't alone, that she had friends. The golden lights were her friends, they were there all the time.

Jung explained to her that we make our own dragons and live with them until we realize that we can break through and find the light, either by ourselves or with the help of others. We can learn to slay our dragons.

Demons, on the other hand, come to us not through our own doing. They are the part of our life experience that has been thrust upon us. Perhaps we inherited a predisposition for an addictive personality, or through no fault of our own, we were raised in an environment of abuse or neglect.

As we journey through life we will encounter shadow figures who come out of our darkness and present themselves.

We must decide whether we created them or were they thrust upon us as part of our life experience. Are they demons or dragons? If they are dragons we must find a way to slay them; if they are demons, we must somehow learn to manage them.

But The Tigers Come at Night

If you are like most people, you work hard all day, crash into bed and hope for a good night's sleep. However, often after a few hours of "sound" sleep, your eyes pop open and the events of the day flood into your head making it impossible to fall back to sleep. The situation compounds itself since you not only have the day's events in your head but you have the added frustration of what a lack of sleep will do to you tomorrow. These tigers come at night and cause many of us to look to sleep aids to eliminate them.

Perhaps there might be another solution. Let me tell you a story.

I had the good fortune of working with a remarkable woman. She helped me with my work in the community and served as a volunteer I could always count on. She was in her nineties and in perfect health. Some of our work required traveling, and during our trips we would engage in fascinating discussions. On one occasion we found ourselves on the topic of sleep, and often the lack thereof.

"Child," she said to me as she would often begin her words to live by, "I have never had any trouble falling back to sleep." As she continued her explanation, I couldn't believe her remedy, it seemed so simple. There were no sleep aids, no soft music, no hypnotism, just an easy mental exercise.

The basic principle is this: even though you may have several ailments, the worst pain is the one you feel. So too with thoughts…you can only have one at a time. She would force her mind to concentrate on one thing, and only one thing.

"I made up a story," she continued, "a fantasy that I would think about whenever my sleep was interrupted. I would keep the story going every night and by doing this, I would always push everything else from my mind, and I would always fall back to sleep."

Sounds simple enough, and when I pressed her to tell her fantasy, she gladly continued. "I placed myself marooned on a desert island with my movie star hero, Clark Gable. We had nothing, no food, water, or shelter. Every time I needed to fall asleep I continued my adventure with Clark. It was as if I was writing a novel and every night was another chapter."

I asked if she and Clark were ever rescued. "Of course not," she exclaimed, "how would I ever get a good night's sleep?"

That was it, a simple mind exercise. So simple, it just might work!

The Ghost Dance

To understand the next power source you will need to step back in time, about 125 years, and relive the experience of the Sioux Indians following their victory at the Battle of the Little Bighorn. After the battle, the tribes were being hunted down and made to relocate onto reservation land. Those who resisted scattered and hid. During this time, the people had to abandon their customary way of life; no longer could they play their drums, sing, dance, and make camp to care for the elders and the very young. Those elements that were the strength of their life were forced underground. Imagine the distance the sound of a drum could travel. Their heartbeat had been silenced and many were forced to take refuge in Canada.

The scattering of the people is a perfect example of a loss of focus, a loss of the centering of a people. On an individual level, Black Elk spoke often of the importance of the vision hoop and in particular, its center.

The retreat to Canada was short-lived. The people missed their homeland and slowly Black Elk, Sitting Bull and their people returned. One by one they began to obey the soldiers and move on to the reservation lands. Their way of life totally changed and they became dependent on the White government for food. They signed treaties that guaranteed them food and other provisions. However, the promises were not kept.

In his report to the Assistant Adjutant-General, Captain J. H. Hurst, Fort Bennett, South Dakota, listed the Indian complaints. Among their grievances the Indians stated that the game had been destroyed and driven out by the White people; that their children were taken from them to eastern schools and kept for years; that the issue of their annuity goods was delayed so late in the winter as to cause much suffering; and that they were expected to plow the land and raise grain when the climate would not permit. His report goes on to state that these issues are well founded and justified by facts.

Reservation life was forced upon them and the Indians, who for their entire lives hunted and followed the buffalo, were now struggling to reconcile themselves to the ways of a new civilization. Hungry, desperate and depressed, Black Elk and his people searched in vain for a center, a focus for their lives. He said, "At that time I could see that the hoop was broken and all scattered out and I thought, I am going to try my best to get my people back into the hoop again."

Then came news of a messiah, a Paiute named Wovoka was teaching about a new religion called the Ghost Dance. Kicking Bear initiated the first Ghost Dance on the Rosebud and Pine Ridge Reservations. Later he went to Standing Rock by invitation of Sitting Bull to inaugurate the dance on that reservation.

Black Elk was excited about this new dance and traveled to Manderson to watch them dance. He saw that it had many of the elements shown to him in his vision. Participants danced in a circle, and in the center was a cottonwood tree. As Black Elk tells us, "they had a sacred pole in the center. It was a circle in which they were dancing and I could clearly see that this was my sacred hoop and in the center they had an exact duplicate of my tree that never blooms and it came to my mind that perhaps with this power the tree would bloom and the people would get into the sacred hoop again." Black Elk found a connection, and perhaps, an opportunity to fulfill the message of his vision given to him so many years before.

Often it is at times of utter despair that we turn inward and find the energy of our center, times when it is least expected and thought impossible. But somehow the energy is tapped, and individuals accomplish the most amazing things.

One might say that the Ghost Dance became everyone's last chance at returning hope in these desperate times. Not being able to change the system, the people had found a way to find their center and yet live within the system, just as Campbell recommended we do. They even agreed to only dance a few times a week. But their intense celebration and the promise of a return to the old ways posed a great threat to the soldiers.

Giving hope, providing a path does empower us. Whether it be on an individual level, or as is the case of Black Elk, on a tribal level, the energizing forces are the same. By connecting to those "ghosts" or that spirit army who has gone before, we have them return to join the effort, to recapture dreams, and to ignite the beacons that were dying. Once again Black Elk's footprints rise up to show us a way, a path toward inner power. A path that leads from "the place where crying begins," to a land where the buffalo again roam free and eagles soar high above the rainbow door.

The Bloody Snow

The Army ordered special investigations to "get to the bottom" of the Ghost Dance movement and the potential Sioux uprising. Like so many other events in history, it was viewed as a "movement" rather than accepted as a religion, and tragedy was near at hand.

On December 15, 1890, Sitting Bull was killed while resisting arrest on the Standing Rock Reservation. Couriers were sent after the fleeing Indians warning them to return to the agency, where they would be safe, or suffer the consequences if found outside the reservation. Within a few days, many had come in and surrendered.

The only prominent leader outside of the Bad Lands who was considered dangerous was Big Foot, whose village was at the mouth of Deep Creek. Big Foot and his band of Minneconjous had fled from the Cheyenne River Reservation on December 23rd to take refuge in the Bad Lands. They were alarmed at the news of Sitting Bull's death and feared the soldiers. Orders had been given to Major Whitside of the Seventh Calvary to intercept Big Foot's party in its flight. On December 28th, Big Foot raised a white flag, and asked for a meeting. Major Whitside refused and demanded an unconditional surrender, which at once was given, and the Indians moved on with the troops to Wounded Knee Creek. In order to make the assurance complete, four additional troops of the Seventh Calvary were added to make a total force of 470 men, as against a total of 106 warriors then present in Big Foot's band.

According to James Mooney's account (1891): On the morning of December 29th preparations were made to disarm the Indians, take them to the agency and then on to the railroad. In obedience to instructions, the Indians had pitched their tipis on the open plain, a short distance west of Wounded Knee Creek. In the center of the camp, the Indians had hoisted a white flag as a sign of peace and a guarantee of safety. Behind them was a dry ravine running into the creek, and on a slight rise in front was posted a battery of four Hotchkiss machine guns, trained directly on the Indian camp. Big Foot himself was ill of pneumonia in his tipi.

Shortly after 8 o'clock in the morning the Indian warriors were ordered to come out of their tipis and deliver their arms. The first twenty went and returned in a short time with only two guns. It seemed evident that they were unwilling to give them up, and so the troops were ordered to search the tipis. After a thorough hunt, about forty rifles were found, most of which were old and of little value. All this searching had its effect on the warriors already wrought up to a high nervous tension and not knowing what might come next. While the soldiers had been looking for the guns, Yellow Bird, a medicine man, had been walking about among the warriors, urging them to resist and telling them that the soldiers would become weak and power-less, and that the bullets would be unavailing against the sacred "ghost shirts" which nearly everyone of the Indians wore. As he spoke in the Sioux language, the officers did not at once realize the dangerous drift of his talk, and the climax came too quickly for them to interfere. Suddenly Yellow Bird stooped down and threw a handful of dust into the air as if it was a signal. A young Indian drew a rifle from under his blanket and fired at the soldiers, who instantly responded with a volley directly into the crowd of warriors. This one volley must have killed nearly half of the warriors. The survivors sprang to their feet, and began a hand to hand struggle. Although many of the warriors had no guns, some had revolvers, knives and clubs. The very lack of guns made the fight more bloody.

At the first volley of the Hotchkiss guns trained on the camp opened fire and sent a storm of shells and bullets among the women and children. The guns poured in 2-pound explosive shells at the rate of nearly fifty per minute, mowing down everything alive. In a few minutes 200 Indian men, women and children with 60 soldiers were lying dead or wounded on the ground. The surviving handful of Indians were running in wild panic to the shelter of the ravine, pursued by hundreds of maddened soldiers and followed up by a ranking fire from the Hotchkiss guns, which had been moved into position to sweep the ravine. Authorities differ as to the number of Indians present and killed at Wounded Knee. General Ruger states that the band numbered about 340, including 100 warriors, the rest women and children.

On New Year's Day, three days after the battle, a detachment of troops had been sent out to Wounded Knee to gather up and bury the Indian dead and to bring in the wounded who might still be alive on the field. In the meantime there had been a heavy snowstorm, culminating in a blizzard. The bodies of the men, women and children were found lying about under the snow, frozen stiff and covered with blood. Almost all the dead warriors were found lying near where the fight began, but the bodies of women and children were scattered along for 2 miles from the scene of the encounter. A number of women and children were found still alive, but all were badly wounded or frozen, or both and most of them died after being brought in. Four babies were found alive under the snow, wrapped in shawls and lying beside their dead mothers, whose last thought had been of them. They were all badly frozen and only one lived. The tenacity of life so characteristic of indigenous people was strikingly illustrated in the case of these wounded and helpless women and children who thus lived three days through a Dakota blizzard, without food, shelter, or attention to their wounds.

Black Elk's account of the tragedy that ensued is accurate. The souls lost in the bloody snow will forever stand as a reminder of their last effort to hold on to the old ways and live as they did for centuries. But for Black Elk, the hope for his people did not end at Wounded Knee. In his lament he called for *Wakan Tanka* to cause their spirits to rise up from the bloody snow and help the old ways to come alive again. His prayer for them is one that asks for the realization of hope and a return to the culture and the value system that was, in fact, their lives.

Excerpt from: The Lost Journal of Tatanka Chante

(Circa 1875), Publication Date: Fall 2011

He was sick. An unknown fever was burning out his strength. For days he could not eat or sleep. Sweat drenched his face. Aching all over he moaned for relief. Everything they gave him didn't work. The doctor said that he would soon die, that there was nothing he could do. Closing his eyes the man fought the pain. Clenching his fists he gritted his teeth; nothing helped. Lying there at this very moment he just wanted to die; as it seemed the only relief.

Outside it was dark and grey. Clouds gathered ominously, billowing upward as if announcing a great storm. High above flashes of lightning and low rumbling thunder echoed through the valley. Soon the rains would come, releasing the unmistakable aroma of a grateful hot earth. Pushed by the swirling wind, the rain began pelting his window, dribbling down in long streaks as if following an invisible finger. Listening to it, the sound reminded him of something he had heard long ago, a drum. Not the kind of drum one hears at military parades, staccato and stately; rather, a drum he heard on one of his military campaigns; muffled, distant.

Leaning back he felt as if a great weight was pressing on his chest, squeezing his heart. Closing his eyes he let it over come him. Swirls of light emanated about and with it the beautiful sound of the distant drums. He wanted to reach out, to go there, to wherever the sounds were. It was exciting; inviting, his heart struggling to burst free.

Then it happened.

He sensed a hand touching him. It was warm and inviting. It felt like his grandfathers hand, a touch he had remembered from his days of long ago. "Grandpa, is that you?"

His hand caressed his sweaty face, wiping away large beads of perspiration. "Who are you?" With tears running down his cheeks as the rain ran down the pane of his window, he waited a response. Keeping his eyes closed, he whispered the words again, "What do you want?" He heard no answer.

It was as if the raging storm outside his window had invaded his very being. Tornado-like, nothing was in place. In the confusing swirl nothing was where it should have been.

The fevered man listened in the chaos for some sound of his name: Jeb....Jeb Tucker. He'd been a soldier, a cavalry trooper, now a Homesteader who had made a quiet living many years working the earth. His wife had passed away a few years ago leaving him with their twins Sarah and Jeremy, now 5 years old.

Jeb Tucker, the old soldier, gloried in those years in the military. Like the storm, war held many dark dangers, but there was excitement too, as only the young in battle can know. Now those days were gone.

He was sick. Could he have stood, he would be bent over and brittle. He had begun feeling like he was a burden to everyone. He had done his duty, made a home, cared for his family, now he was lying in an old cabin, crippled with fever. But the presence he felt was friendly, almost fatherly. Reaching up he touched the hand. It felt warm.

For the first time he opened his eyes. What he saw amazed him. Standing above him was an Indian, a man about his own age. He was dressed in fine buckskin. Down the front of his shirt were beaded trappings in a blaze of brilliant colors. Grey hair enfolded his face chiseled with strong features; and the eyes. He could never forget the eyes. The eyes were friendly, sparkling with intelligence and delight.

    Suddenly he felt a wave coursing through him. Far away he heard those drums, not so distant now; and yes, yes, he could hear people singing, Indian people singing to the beat of that muffled drum, and in the singing he heard was not just the tribal songs of an ancient people, but the unmistakable sound of his very own name. In the midst of the wind and the thunder, he felt his body rise upward. As he traveled through the clouds, he turned and saw that Sarah and Jeremy were with him. Surprisingly they were not afraid. Finally they came to a calm and quiet place, full of light. The grandfather spoke, "Your pain is gone and your suffering is over forever."

    Now my two little ones, there is special work for you. You are to return to the living world as you are changed into children's dolls. Sarah, you will be named *Conala Wigmunke Chante*, which means Little Rainbow Heart. The children will simply call you Chante. You, Jeremy, will be known as *Conala Tatanka*, Little Buffalo.

    Terrible times about to come to the Indian people. Their lives will change forever and it will be very difficult for them to survive. You must be there to help the little children live through these times.

    You see, when a child is born, it leaves the spirit world, but it does not leave alone. Spirits go with the children and give them gifts to keep them safe and strong. These gifts are filled with mystical power that comes from ancient mysteries. The people of the Ghost Dance knew of this power and called upon it when they were in trouble.

    However, as children do, they begin to attach themselves to the world of the living and lose the ability to hear the spirits.

That is why you both must keep a journal to record the nature of the gifts and the power given to the children. This will be very important for future generations who will also face terrible times of their own and no longer listen to the spirits. The gifts of the old ways point to the power and energy they will need.

You will return on the cloud that brought you, and do not be afraid. (To be continued.)

Behold the Earth, For across it are Two Roads

With these words, the fourth grandfather in Black Elk's great vision told of the two roads in life that a person can choose between. The black road (also called blue) is a fearful road that runs from where the sun shines continually to where the sun goes down (east and west), and it is the road of the Thunder-beings. "Behold the black road for it shall be a fearful road. With this road you shall defend yourself."

He went on to say, "behold the sacred red road that runs from where we always face to where the giant is (north and south). This road shall be your nation, from this road you shall receive the power to do good." The red road is the good or straight way for the north is purity and the south is the source of life. The red road is similar to the Christian "straight and narrow way"; it is the vertical of the cross. Black Elk tells us that red represents all that is sacred, especially the earth, for we should remember that it is from the earth that our bodies come and it is to her that they return.

In terms of our personal journey, the Red Road represents a choice or direction for us to go. If we examine Maslow's higher levels of need, specifically self-realization, the need for confidence and self-worth. Concentration on our inner self will point the way to who we are and the potential of what we really can become. This final steps in our journey across the bridge leads us to the most critical step, one that involves an even higher level of need: self-actualization.

Maslow goes into great detail in describing the self-actualizing person. He said that the self-actualizing person enjoys solitude and privacy, particularly as it relates to a sense of security and self-sufficiency. Self-actualizing persons are more aware of their environment, both human and nonhuman. They have a high level of acceptance of self, others and nature. Self-actualizing persons are not ashamed or guilty about their human nature, with its shortcomings, imperfections, frailties, and weaknesses. Nor are they critical of these aspects in other people. They respect and esteem themselves and others. Self-actualizing persons repeatedly experience awe, pleasure, and wonder in their everyday world. In varying degrees, they have feelings of wonder with limitless horizons opening up, followed by a conviction that the experience was important and must carryover into everyday life. They have a deep feeling of empathy, sympathy, and compassion for human beings in general. Most important, this feeling is unconditional. And finally, the self-actualizing person is highly ethical and willing to learn from anyone.

One might say that the Red Road is actually the road to self-actualization. Campbell mentioned the special place as being our "bliss station" but in terms of our personal fulfillment, the goal is to journey forward on a path that is waiting for us. The fourth grandfather called the Red Road the path of peace and harmony and so it is. By finding your center and realizing who you are, you are now ready to travel forward and put action into your dream, or as Campbell tells us, follow your bliss.

We are not alone, Campbell continues, for every inch along the way we are helped by "hidden hands." Doors will open, he says, doors that you never knew were there. If you follow your bliss, you'll have that joy and that refreshment you need all the time.

Two on a Bridge

He uses the analogy of an umbilical cord to signify the lifeline aiding us as we travel out from our center and journey along the road we will travel. It is our connection to what is real for us. The world is constantly trying to distract us with occasional concerns, but holding to this umbilical cord helps us to deal with life's everyday issues, a technique one has to work out for one's self. But he promises, sooner or later we'll find the capacity that's waiting to be awakened and will lead us to this other place. It is there you will learn to recognize your own depths, where the deep sense of being informed is felt, a place where your soul and body want to go.

But as with most elements of our lives, the destination is secondary. It is the journey that most involves us. How we travel through our days, as well as the direction we choose to take are really most important.

Two on a Bridge: The Guideposts

One principle is certain, if you step on to the bridge and follow its guideposts, you will not be the same person who steps off at the end.

Maintain your own special place, a base location just for you alone. Your meditation here will begin with a certain state of mind, a level of awareness which will eventually lead itself to its own energy source.

Maintain a consistent place to meet with your partner. As this place becomes more familiar, it will eventually produce a power source of its own.

After each meeting with your partner, return to your own special place for reflection.

Two on a Bridge

Think of your life as a circle containing all the elements of your world both positive and negative.

Throughout your day your must constantly decide whether or not an issue is a positive or negative force. If it is positive keep it close to you and nourish it. If it is negative, try not to concentrate on it, this gives it energy and strength.

You will never be totally free from negative forces. There will always be demons invading your circle. Do our best to recognize them for what they represent, and keep them as far from your center as possible.

When you are not in your special place, remember the positive thoughts and call on them when you need a burst of energy and joy.

You must learn to manage your demons, because some of them will always exist. But you must slay your dragons because you are the one who created them.

When you are alone, concentrate on your feelings, develop an inner focus that reveals a central point inside of you. This energy source is found by your heart, not your head.

The power doesn't necessarily come from those who have died, rather it comes from the belief in the power of the connection.

Belief helps us to understand that there is an invisible plain behind the visible one, supporting us with energy. Faith is designed to put our mind in accord with our body and our way of life in accord with the way nature designs.

Repression protects the negative forces, the shadows from vanishing, because repressed feelings have the very best chance of survival, as we know from experience that nothing is corrected in the unconscious. The shadows just remain dormant until your energy level is exhausted and they find their way back into your thoughts.

CPSIA information can be obtained at www.ICGtesting.com
Printed in the USA
BVOW070012041011

272673BV00001B/2/P